How Much We Must Have Looked Like Stars To Stars

New Women's Voices Series, No. 126

To Rachel,

The world may be on fire
but fire purifies. The world
that we create is greater than the
one we leave behind.

poems by

Alysia Nicole Harris

Finishing Line Press
Georgetown, Kentucky

How Much We Must Have Looked Like Stars To Stars

New Women's Voices Series, No. 126

ACKNOWLEDGMENTS

Warm & grateful acknowledgements are given to the editors of the publications
in which the following poems appeared first in sometimes slightly varied forms:

Adanna Literary Journal: "Ishmael", "True & Legitimate Wife"
Catch & Release: Migration
Indiana Review: "Moths on Loan"
Print Oriented Bastards: "Famine"
Solstice Literary Magazine: "Crow's Sugar", "Omnipotence"
Squaw Valley Review: "Spigot"
Vinyl Magazine: "The Murderess"

Publisher: Leah Maines

Editor: Christen Kincaid

Cover Art and Design: Marilyn Murray

Author Photo: Kevin Watkins

Printed in the USA on acid-free paper.
Order online: www.finishinglinepress.com
also available on amazon.com

Author inquiries and mail orders:
Finishing Line Press
PO Box 1626
Georgetown, Kentucky 40324
USA

Table of Contents

PENTECOST

—after Elena Shumilova

the snout of it reaches out & curls
towards me panting, breath
condensing on my bating hands—
churchfolk say that's
the Spirit—its paws
looming like a great
bear in my blindness & detected
only by the primal hairs
on the back of my neck
which shout
one at a time
like women in pews
& then all at once

VOTIVE

*[The women undulate their voices so as to paint a blue coat
upon the back of grief.]*

Every day I don't swim in myself is a day where I keep your name
on high ground. A smile above my hips that can melt snow, catch
sun.

What grass did you braid into my hair that evening under the
cantaloupe sky? Only night breathes between us & a few
dismembered flecks of light...how much we must have looked
like stars to stars.   It's true. You don't usually see cicadas
in cities. Their hatching ground paved over. For three weeks
the soil squirms under the street. Then goes inert—a layer
alive, a layer dead.

How belief sounded before before? Oh, Babylon fit in a thimble.

Outside to the left was a well of children, whose bones curved
like the first question. Yes,   we are that ancient.

Where my skin breaks I feel stretched by love's tires, like a
tapestry of roadkill. Do the women still sing songs about it?

Solitude is the only salvation I've ever heard of
where the savior & the saved are the same.

There is no call for rescue distinct from the answer.
You thought you were safe. You didn't know
you were sacred here.

Your name snagged on my breath. Every time I mentioned you
the fence rattled. For two months I tried to be a prison. Tried
to keep you here, the way evidence keeps a crime alive. Then
love caught me by the chin & started eating my ear. Its voice
rang clear, had hardly any distance to it. *This is how you make*

love: you devour everything. You don't throw up after.

I kiss you lavishly

simply;

every adulteress has her stone.

The first time we knew we were alive, it was pain that told us.

The only knowledge I have to give of me is words. Each syllable constructs one side of a fence. Meaning, a yard I run through a hundred times over until I am stained & skinned from the waist down. I lay in the middle of my language like a dog that dragged itself home. An exhibit without doors.

Each of its murders in a working brain.
The alphabet is full of little knives

                                     & the world is a zoo.
All it takes is something as inexcusable as glass to make the whole thing lionproof. My mom hacked the limbs off the Christmas tree then went outside & cut down her favorite shrub in the yard which had busted under the weight of snow. *This is how you keep the dead dead.* The middle exposed a swamp of spider webs.

When did I become this cruel nightmare? Did the glass glow like
    honey?
Were your dozing hands still knotted in my hair…the strands,
    digits, the years made out of two's & zero's

until everything was old.

If time were paralyzed like so it would move like a skinned cobra & we would drink the poison from under its fangs until all we did was shake like midnight through leaves.

I have cast nets of you, lots of you, dice of you & turned up with six shining faces. Each more unquestionable & terrible than the next, like a Babylonian god. I bring you my lips, my passport, my favorite verse from Song of Solomon, my dress that smells of smoke.

& I don't care if it doesn't make sense because this is how I throw my weight around. Without you the world so grieves & excites me

I am certain I will die from it. Of course, I will.

In my dream last night we lived in a slum. But there you were, with sunflowers, vodka, a parcel of fresh salmon, threating to make everything alive.

I cannot say desire five times without it once being true. There was blood coming from my nose when I left you.

THE STORM HAD A WOMB FROM WHERE THE BIRDS LEAPT

I planted our infidelity in lavender,
in musket-blue, into the indigo of his wife's innocent face.

The mistress can always identify the wife
by the eyes but the wife will never know mine.

Isn't that the point? A pleasure so clandestine
it doesn't exist. Whatever smell is more verdant than sweat, pretend

it is eternal. Eternally, I'm a dead bird
repenting its feathers to the pope of gravity—

Barely even notice it's my blood
staining violets in his hands—Once,

I felt a flock of waxwings in
my veins. Once I was a kite

at the vanishing point. He & I looked like petals
torn from the bouquet in a lover's hand.

Paralyzed acrobat, I sat, for the last time,
bovine in the fields & watched my nipples sour

under my clothes,
rain making a slaughterhouse of everything

& him, loving me slow & steady like day
coming on in a swollen sky. Once I was

the darted gaze, the pregnant
pause before the pitying

of marriage doves. Once
I was so big with love.

FIRST WORSHIP

The valley wailing
against the window. Greens, peach,
the olivewine leaves gathered
like so many
breaths. Could anything else start
out simple &
over time accumulate such
contours?

Does anything else preach? The road a line, the line a cobweb,
the cobweb a stretch of light, the light a mask &

once we were
on the other side of it,
Creation
kicked. My chest was still a far harvest, a plain of pale
unpicked
Shenandoah squash
growing

slow & womanly
in the slanted sun.

My body is linked to this place through the gut. So no,

I don't
cover my head when I worship. The ground
& my body, already flush.

MOTHS ON LOAN

A butterfly can be a quarter
female & 3/4ths   male.
When you have perfect bilateral symmetry
it's just simpler to divide. In some cases

the patterning can be deceptive.
You must   examine the genitalia
to be sure
who's who, if you know what I mean.
                          Under my wound cocoon
of   cotton & fleece
& down bedding, metal blue on one side,
a weak brown on the other,
I crack my thighs
                          & ruffle the hair
on my quarter part. There's nothing gorgeous or
neutral to halve me.   For a butterfly

it's easy.
One brighter wing. One bigger wing.
Poor thing
probably flies in circles.

        But I've no torrid spots   or garish orange
nothing as exact as a moth's   needle-wide & barely
there.   You must handle

                        the specimens
with due care otherwise you'll tear
the wings & you'll be
left
with   feelers, thorax, abdomen,
gender. I leave

myself on the window screen at night &   try
to summon mates. I loose my curls,
my organs
        swell & bleed—I need a spear
to tell me this is a hole.

        & sometimes if the wind
is right,   I read Lorca in the Spanish
        until I'm feminine
enough to sleep.

APOLOGIES ARE NOT ANTI-VENOM

I dreamt your veins last night.
They melted like sugar in my mouth.

I swore you were warming up to me or was that just the after-
glow of vodka making my guts feel pretty.

I promise I didn't mean to wake you. It's just the drunk
monsters know your number better than anyone.

§

Are apologies labors of sweat? Should I salt them
from my brow then build us an underwater reef

or merely admit I'm human?
& no, that's not an excuse,

just meant to say egotism is an easy tide,
& I've never known a shark to be selfless.

§

I'll tell the next man, *Stranger,*
my love went forfeit a long time ago, so don't

expect me to spread like some unsteady
bridge when the blade of your tongue cuts

the arch of my back & London falls
all around us, I won't

rebuild, just evaporate like the last
time you & I settled for making love instead of making peace.

You left me sobbing, dripping like a question mark
so full of beg. I still wonder what

you know about drowning & water births and
if you ever found your sea legs.

As often as I've gone on vacation
I've witnessed a funeral:

seen women run behind coffins,
breaking a sweat from their eyes,

stood exiled in an orthodox church outside Moscow
caught between the dead man & the door, trying not to stare

at the corpse like a tourist. Every vacation,
a death, a wake. So each time I'm tempted

to get away with my words, I'm reminded
every poem is a tombstone,

§

eulogizing a moment. Our introduction
took the shape of a sonnet. I only had 10 syllables

to learn your name, didn't bother to tell you mine,
just ended the couplet:

Signed,
Your slave.

The first poem I wrote paired fire & desire
out of necessity. I learned 173 ways to rhyme with *Please*!

I tried to buy you a victrola off e-bay.
That was the easiest way for me to say I'm sorry.

I only scratched our records so they
repeated at all the good parts

        but please, do not find me in that dream again,
                caramelized by your mouth.

§

        Dust huddles on the edge of our numbered photographs,
        love in 2 dimensions. I gather each little stillness to me

                like a clutch of precious eggs. If I fracture
        all over the floor. Who will sweep me into myself?

One day I will be 37 minutes widowed,
repeating in the odd quiet of being married but not,

"I was young till I was old."
How do we stumble upon death?

§

        Suddenly we find it, close as a nightstand's
        edge in the dark. The Anatomy of an ache

             where the hurt is punctual each time.
                      I am sorry

             I still search for the one apology
              to be the anti-venom I need.

        I fold the photo album around me like your arms
        after each counted year, dim the reading lights

& let the joy of never feeling the same way twice
open me like a novel.

MIGRATION

Or fear.
This crane-heart
buckles like a train. My chest
becomes a mobile cage,
a spinning gibbet
when it traverses
a suspension
bridge. The nesting
waters below, a heaven
so cold it creaks, so
you'd think the river
had bones & just bones,
hands without palms
from which we sop
blood or cup blood—
the seat a dead sea
I can lay lengthwise
in. Windows
model then shed
every landscape:
twin wheat fields,
shipping yard of exiled color,
this cruel breath—My eyes close
to leave the argument
like California smiling
on a map. Shifting
my weight, I resettle
to where the ground gives up
a fetus, to where the train retracts
like a tongue into the dark's
mouth—The names
I can't say. The names I won't
say. Staring down the past
at the future separately
through each eye, I

call to the dead. & the
dead, they
comfort me; I breathe
their breath. I will not curse
in front of life tonight.

OMNIPOTENCE

She got sick even though the moon is supposedly everyone's nightlight. I thought, *Nessun dorma.* My heart banged down the stairs like an anvil.

The sex in Venice tore open the curtains before dawn. Against your abdomen, my pelvis feels like a crucible. Say anything serious like chemo & I'll respond with the follow up: *Why don't we move to Egypt & buy a bunch of camels? Why don't we kick in the doctor's teeth?*

She looks like Pavarotti on stage sweating under the lights. She is all in her feelings, meaning it is for her survival. No... you definitely can't translate the book of Jeremiah with a mouth full of painkillers but I've watched her sing. & sweat straight through my blazer, the one borrowed for the show she had to cut her hair like a boy's. While you sleep in the big Venetian bed, I try the blazer on, unwashed months later, sitting in the balm of her clothes:

Fire tornadoes in Brazil make blind men see. Ice on the other hand, is a small miracle. All she needs is a small miracle.

She & I are back in Luxor, & the mangoes are holding the bruise of youth green to their skin. You never think of the mosquitoes present in the soil, hunting the air, skirting along the water.
You don't think that mosquitoes will bite your feet till you can't walk, so swollen & full is the fruit.

I tell you she is ill, & you hang me over your big arms & soothe me with geneticist words. You make me wet when you talk about hell this way. Except the lover you are pales next to the sex I had in Luxor, which was not sex really but a mango opened by the machete. I asked for the pit too. The half that was my sex, I kissed out with juice-stung face till I was crying & stoning myself at the same time.

I. THE MURDERESS

After repeated stays due to evidence of torture &
coercion Iran Human Rights confirms, a woman prisoner
Safieh "Maryam" Ghafouri was hanged early this morning.
— *Shiraz, Iran, July 12, 2012*

They led her, burqa & blindfold, in. They (masc. pl.)
executed the mother, Mary.
No scaffold/ elegant gallows. Instead
an industrial crane, all spine & faultless height,

hanged her like an outdoor chandelier that shines no light;
her garments barely tripped the wind.
Lovely lute-corseted birds hung in painted cages, all Vermeer's
tiny women too, sing a song for Maryam Ghafouri.

all false? adulteresses
lick burning stones
innocent witches sink,   *iron thrones*
On the sill, our pearls, portraits, scales

sit for Muses. O, Exonerated Queen of Heaven,
we'll kill the hounds with handguns.

II. THE SONGSTRESS

Now, Rihanna opens up to Oprah. Plus, find out why
Rihanna felt protective of Chris despite her anger.

I am Ishtar, idol to many, yet keep only one:
my Baal of ballers. His closed fist

chested within my smaller closed fist.
I confess, upon the priestess' couch,

Music's Odalisque of Grief, the pendulous
bell inside me still rings. The songs I've sung for him,

the tears to sing. I miss his hands
open or closed. Like hot stones, they massage.

In this hopeless place I sprawl millions,
dollars about my feet—Even diamonds have a sex.

Dolls with noses designed for snow. Here Gabbana,
There, myrrh—*Don't you know the gifts we give?*

From the mongrel heart, drug my dead young to the throne room.
I'm his bottom bitch as long as he likes the view.

III. TRUE & LEGITIMATE WIFE

> *I would rather be a poor beggar's wife & be sure of,*
> *heaven, than queen of all the world & stand in doubt*
> *thereof by reason of my own consent.*
> —Katharine of Aragon, Queen of England

A nun's clothes are too modest for grief;
I want the show. Alone in a cell
I pray for rescue but rest assured

I need no pope to confer my peace. No matter what is said,
I never polluted my womb. Belly a catholic place,
my almost sons slept on clean blood pillows

though my heart sits atop a tiny staircase
that I know will break. Look how the whore & bastard
gained his grace, boasting my death. Like canaries

some brave women go to the grave donning gold
so I will not wear a widow's robes,
sleeved in black, old tooth of poison. My blood,

dark, dark fountain, leaves me in streams
to wash his feet. Goodbye eats all my air—
he'll need more than prayer to charm his sleep.

IV. ISHMAEL

She gave this name to The Lord who spoke to her:
"Hai Roi," for she said, "I have now seen the One
who sees me."

—*Genesis 16:13*

Each mother squats & badmouths the sky: God,
it is easy to raise the son, from a throne. But who
without full belly can stomach their own eclipse?

The daughter-self quits the mother-self
to warn her—
The feeding happens in the blood.

Magnificent Sarah, master with the withered womb,
slaved for children till she was out of stillborns.
Slave-girl wished herself rid of sand, of bastard sobs;

Egypt in her reed-arms. Hagar walked
a desert, no milk in her breasts & yet
matriarch to a guttural cry.

Strength is a shared sigh. There are only used names for
daughters, like Self. Borrowed
from inside the waters of Adam.

The child of promise is *he who laughs* but *he*, a biology that never
   mourns.
The women howl & call each other Ishmael, finally first-born.

WAKE

—for Sabrina Fulton, mother of Travyon Martin &
Lesley McSpadden, mother of Michael Brown

After the death of her baby, what will give her
the botanical sleep of plants if prozac
wasn't made for people of color,
& not even a stomach full of xanax
can quiet her dreams, which are now
a legion, & she,
the demoniac, whom Jesus empties if he can
empty
that grief. The body performs
many exorcisms in life but none like birth.
The tether is umbilical unto the soul,
such that out of it is grafted
an individually-new crop,
& if it should be cut down, if it should be
murdered,
the mother, without fail, will become a shadow
or perhaps, a fossil, like a mussel
put to the lips & sucked out,
body between someone else's teeth. & that someone keeps
swallowing.
Out of habit. Long after the sea-taste
is undetectable. The murderer keeps swallowing
cups of coffee, keeps cutting purple
geraniums for his wife who never suspects
the boy might have had a favorite color,
that his favorite color might have been
purple. This couple sleeps in peace
as if peace doesn't need to be paid for—you have no idea
what some people pray for: your rhubarb pies
to come out burnt, your next child to be stillborn,
all the ribs in your chest
snapped with a bolt cutter—Nothing is too much,
no wished suffering in this silence which picks
its teeth. A mother can clean

her dead son's room but can't throw anything
out: each picture gathered to her bed, an unwashed
little league uniform, a favorite pair of boots
scuffed, bought half a size too big
so he'd still have room to grow, the gold
herringbone chain for his 12th
birthday, his first A. There they lie
rudely strewn about—she's ready to swim
or drown. All around her,
her boy un-buoyant
& unlike water, unable to rise.

FAMINE

I want to say what was soft & saccharine
I've eaten from your marrowed honeycomb.
To the daughter, the mother is
already a ghost. I can see through
her translucent ears.
That makes me the weed

& not the desiderata. Daisies or lilies you won't find;
everything's already been milked. There's no need to talk,
to put a bucket under the udders & pray for rain.
When a sow bites she might take
a finger. When it's a whip-spider
she might take your eyes. She might add to her panopticon
your soft-brown telescopes. I have done this to you
& not given thanks. Mother,

the body you've given me has been mine
for over two decades. I have used it to erase you
so fight back. Draw the angle like a scythe through time,
cut the first flowering of my oleander bones.
Someone should have told you

a child will suck your sun. I am sorry
I have only ever loved you in an excess of guilt,
though you gave me many titles for the inside of your palm:
my back door into church,
my bristle brush, & snot rag.
You, woman who cut the crust off
my white bread, let me lay across your lap.
Let's dream we are both young. We are
both young at the same time. We are there now,
back when you still sunbathed,
when you were not angry with my father,
before your hair was braided back for war—

I am 4000 miles from the place
where you are more than just a word. I cannot go
to sleep in my heart. I wet everything & let
parts of me disappear in the drain.
They leave me to crawl homeward,
to the good earth
to your pelvic bowl, to the draw
from which you ladled out the small

bullion of my life. Mother, I won't burn
though you leave me on the stove all day.
Mother, I'm only water. It's okay
if some of it drains. Let us be famished awhile.
I want to feed you from my own mouth.

FEAR OF AGING

My batted eye, my pretty please isn't what it used to be:
          no longer the trump card or fake
ID on a Thursday night for the girl I left

at the bar inside me & guessed would still be there
          having another drink. I remember her movements,
the fastening & unfastening,

the quit clothes. How nothing collapsed.
          But now a strange slowness
mires my limbs. The body says no,

again & again, petitioning the heart
          to languish like a horse
inside a burnt-down barn, scenting

over scorched apples, a dumb animal who can't forget
          where there once was sweetness. Pull the girl's anatomy
from your mind. Now a sag. Now a shift.

A man won't want to
          press his lips to it. The slow joke of beauty
is gravity & repetition. Nothing stays just so—

the rise of a skirt might one day involve
          a scaling of sorts. A lace bra to the floor
is also the ground lifting.

CROW'S SUGAR
—for Ibrahim

I stole a watermelon from your kitchen. I must've been about 18.
I'm thinking of a black-eyed angel.

The other boys said you wasn't worth your salt if you wasn't
tasting me. I hid my virginity under my shirt & that summer

we sang like we had azaleas bottlenecked in our throats.
When we'd catch a storm, our laundry swung

on the muscular thunder.
Rigor or love in our small fingers—a sweet sort of choking.

The squash, the corn, sweeter than antifreeze—I must've been
about 18. I was full of your seed, & the lavender came down
    like a motorcade.

That summer God told me stars used to be audible.
Does it have to be a full six octaves of guns between us?

A piece of me is corroded. Is submerged.

Stars hit high notes. Ella & everybody up there,
throwing our heads back, letting the howl bloom upright—

They told me drown your name in the third chorus of Ave Maria.
Nobody told me to call the crows Sugar.

I must have been about 18.
Back pew bridge to sorrow, wailing

if you wasn't tasting me on clean linen on newly tarred roads
if you wasn't teasing me out on a string.

Ella & everybody up there wailing, *I'm thinking of a black eyed*
angel, dope boy in the attic. Marry me! I am full of your seed.

Once I stole a watermelon from your kitchen.
You poured salt on & ate to the rind.

A piece of me is corroded. Leaves a stain of beets
between my lips sweeter than antifreeze on newly tarred roads,

the lavender came down like a motorcade in spring.

My body was a carcass. You poured salt on
& ate to the rind. But wasn't there syrup once?

Wasn't it sound, rigor or love? In our small hands
crickets shuck the night & leave their skin.

My body was a carcass. Ella & everybody up there wailing.
A sweet sort of choking.

I'm thinking of a black-eyed angel, the dope boy in the attic

innocent as Anne, as a wolf under the moon. Stars hit high notes.
A full six octaves of guns. Wasn't it sound?

I hid my virginity under my shirt. A stain of beets on our laundry
after hunting with revolvers, kneading the dead through soil.

Sweeter than antifreeze. I am
full of your seed.

I must have been about 24.
Nobody told me to call the crows Sugar.

This summer a whale, finchlike, eats from the uncoiled knot
    of my hand.

THE GREEK WORD FOR DISPLACEMENT OR THE BODY OF THE WIFE DURING DEPLOYMENT

After you left, I spent a lot of time staring at the hair bumps, which collected like peppercorns on the backs of my legs. Fanatical in my pruning, I was Sir Thomas Moore of ripping things up by the root. I stopped looking for myself in myself. I was not there. I was in the kitchen washing two glass-mouthed bottles. I was in the mirror, am the chess set with the missing piece, pawn on the fire-escape, the answering machine where your disembodied voice is kept alive for months.

When you returned, the time you spent with me was furious, tedious, & like masturbation, gracious toward the body. I spend much more time these days reading essays on suffering. I have learned that ecstasy is the Greek word for displacement. Like masturbation, the words want to be touched, so much so that I've made a space inside the suffering:

> *ecstasy*: such severe pleasure that when the eyes roll
> back in the skull they cease to be windows &
> become widows, spinsters fluttering behind a
> locked door—such severe pleasure that once my heart
> had severed from my body, been torn out & gulped
> by eagles, smiles creased my lips, & some believe
> that I could be heard muttering strange words, repeating
> psalms, saying thank you.

SPIGOT

Trying to breathe with my head
outside the car window, eyes shut
against the speed with which everything moves, I cling
to this one immutable form—

Galaxy Spout, Glittering Mohawk of Stars,
               Cut-Into-The-Old-Bucket-Of-Space,
                       wash me like a palomino. My legs ache
        for a stillness. The stars
        are good & dead
even when they are visible. I am not

                      like the rocks, which are pros
             at being reborn
    smaller
& smaller with the years.
        I'm just this size
      which hurts. My body's been colored in
with a leaden tip.

I have acquired only skinny wisdom,
a dirt-stray-ravaged sort of thinking,
descending deeply into the lightless cools, led
by the blood smell, dark & polished
as a nickel in water—

      Is it grief or the intimacy of grief that draws me here?

           One day I want to rise the way an albatross
    comes up
        for air.

FEAST WITH OUR BODIES ON THE TABLE

We ate yellow kimchi & read
Neruda like swans in heat
the nights we had lovers lay against
our mossless bodies, each a naked stone.
Moans, O's that stretched their smoke
into the night & the
pleasure that collaborated,
gossip as much as gospel.

We each wore heels,
just as told, with legs spread as they
flashed pictures. The camera
swallowed our skin half
a dozen times. It felt good
to be picked & be picked clean;
we didn't know.
A blotch on the breast
means owned as easily as it means
loved. Placed like a diadem

the heat lounged over us,
congregated beneath our sweltering
amplitudes. This was the heaven
we read. We were still young, &
it was still painful. Our cunts itched
from all the humping—our throats
greased & stuffed like ducks. No
water, uh-un, we still wanted
watches to wait for our first
to return with promises & perhaps
even flowers.

Missing him was luxurious
like the sourness of green wine
in winter. Each of us had a him
who glutted our bellies, till summer
ran down the corners of our lips.

IT BURNS WHEN YOU TOUCH IT

A ghost horde of ex-lovers perfumed & giant as the tropics hovers over & kisses me with one mouth.

Lord, it's very likely my genitals will incite the next coup that bars me from your pure plastic sanctioned heaven.

Desire is a drawstring, & the brain is a gigantic balloon one must catch & tether to marrow.

During the late hours I doubted in the tub that my heart was real. I could put blood in it but could not cultivate iron. I can cry tears for the legless but cannot cry down legs.

The Soul that inhabits finds me flammable. *Humor us,* the ghost lovers say. *Taste our hands like licorice on the small of your back*—I keep telling God I need a do-over.

If my anatomy has been staged, maybe it's because my Spirit, hungry for the next incarnation, ate through my bones.

If the plastic of heaven burns, I am now sure the moon begs for the feel of water, the shock of it against her pale big toe.

Like, when I touch me, pleasure like a wired thing. But what do You know of longing? This body You've given me has so many holes.

Is it a crime to fill even one, Lord?
How else should I float?

SHARPNESS EXPERIENCED AS LUMINOSITY OR SENSITIVITY TO COLD
—*after Elena Shumilova*

Light slides its old feet over a newly paved road.
Its closed eyes have opened tirelessly
over a billion times on the same still
barely visible body. I don't want

to die every day. Again I have needs
without words for them. The window
places a nipple of cold in my mouth;
I'm alive in the way that plants are alive

& without tears. I suckle the light
the water, the cold
water wolfishly, operating each
of the painful teeth.

God, spare me the serenity.
Grant me each serrated edge.

Alysia Nicole Harris is an internationally-known performance artist and poet hailing from Alexandria, Virginia. She is a Cave Canem fellow, founding member of the performance poetry collective, The Strivers Row, and co-founder of the start-up Artist Inn Detroit. Alysia has toured nationally and internationally in Canada, Germany, Slovakia, South Africa, and the UK and has spoken at the United Nations. She performs her poems with an eye towards healing and sees her work as promoting transparency, a guilt-free spirituality, women's empowerment and racial reconciliation.

Two time Pushcart nominee, and two-time winner of the 2015 and 2014 Stephen Dunn Poetry Prize, Alysia's poems have appeared in *Indiana Review, Solstice Literary Magazine, Vinyl,* and *Best New Poets 2015.* Her work has been anthologized in *The BreakBeat Poets: New American Poetry in the Age of Hip-Hop.* In 2015, she was also selected as the Duncanson Artist-in-Residence at the Taft Museum of Art in Cincinnati.

Alysia completed her MFA in poetry at NYU and her PhD in linguistics at Yale University. She currently lives in Atlanta, Georgia where she participates in various organizations dedicated to the revitalization of the literary arts in the South.

CPSIA information can be obtained
at www.ICGtesting.com
Printed in the USA
LVHW092106200319
611338LV00001B/122/P